# CRANKY THE CAT

TEXT AND ILLUSTRATIONS BY
SHIRLEY READ-JAHN

SR-J PUBLICATIONS

*For Chiara and Caspar*

# CONTENTS

Cranky the cat was cranky, bad-tempered in all ways, or so everyone said. Nobody liked Cranky. From the moment she woke up in the morning, she had a sour look on her black and white whiskery face. She was an unhappy kitty.

"How did you get that way?" asked Mrs. Catzenpfeffer, her owner. "You've got a comfortable bed, water, lots of lovely fish to eat. Are you sick? I wonder why you are so darned CRANKY?"

"I'm not bad-tempered, it's just that my eyebrows are too close to my nose and make me look angry," meowed Cranky to Mrs. Catzenpfeffer.

"Nobody understands me. Maybe I should just go away and hide under a bush where no-one can find me." Cranky slipped through the cat-door and out into the garden.

Oh, but all those beautiful flowers to sniff! She went from plant to plant, her whiskers twitching with delight as she pressed her nose against all the brightly-coloured blooms in her own little garden.

Hungry for her breakfast, Cranky slid back through the cat-door and into the kitchen. As Mrs. Catzenpfeffer placed a bowl of tuna on the floor for the little cat, Cranky whacked at her hand, scratching her old owner.

"Ow, you horrible little pussy cat!" yelled the old lady, "You're so naughty!"

Cranky curled up on a yellow pillow in a corner with her paws over her green eyes. She felt sorry for herself. A fly buzzed into the room and hovered over the little cat, taunting her.

Cranky loved batting at flies. She was good at catching them. Peering through the five toes on her front paw, she watched and waited, then suddenly sprang up in one flying motion, caught the fly, then fell to the ground, all four legs splayed out from her body. Mrs. Catzenpfeffer roared with laughter.

"Well, you do make me laugh from time to time, you funny little kitty, so you're not all bad."

The old lady started pounding her dough for the day's bread, banging her closed fist into the mixture, humming loudly off-key as she worked. Cranky didn't like the banging noises or the tuneless song. She jumped up onto a kitchen chair, reached over to her owner, lifted a paw, this time scratching Mrs. Catzenpfeffer on her wrist.

"That should stop that annoying noise you're making," Cranky hissed.

"Ouch, you nasty, bad cat! That hurt, you hot-tempered animal, you! Why do you do things like that?"

Cranky slunk away, jumped off the kitchen table and ran outside again.

Admiring her favourite flowers, she saw a yellow snake with a green head slithering out of sight, but it wasn't quick enough for the cat. She dived under the bush, grabbed the snake and gave it a great shake. She then took her prize into the kitchen to show it off to her owner. Mrs. Catzenpfeffer was horrified.

"Get that snake out of my kitchen. It could bite me, or you, it's obviously not dead, you silly little cat!"

Cranky stood still, the snake dangling from her mouth, her whiskers quivering above it.

Turning around, she marched back outside and tossed the snake into the garden pond, where it regained its senses and quickly swam off, leaving S-shaped trails in the water.

Cranky heard a noise, turned around and noticed an orange tomcat sitting atop the garden fence, looking haughtily down upon her.

Cranky sat herself down upon the ground, with one leg stuck high up in the air, and preened the fur on her lower body. She pretended to ignore the other cat, but all the time kept a wary eye on him. Tommy the tomcat puffed out his chest and continued to glare down upon the little black and white cat.

Cranky lowered her leg, put her head thoughtfully to one side, then suddenly dashed up to the fence. In one bound she was up next to Tommy, arching her back, snarling and hissing. She gave his face a sharp whack, claws drawn.

Tommy responded in kind and soon the two animals were down on the ground, rolling, hissing, and fighting hard, as the dirt flew out in all directions around them.

Hearing the commotion, Mrs. Catzenpfeffer ran outside, waving her wooden spoon, her hands still covered in flour.

"Leave that tomcat alone, Cranky, you disagreeable feline!"

Cranky ran off under a bush to lick the wounds Tommy had given her. She stayed under the bush for an hour, dozing and thinking. She pondered on her behaviour, concluding that maybe she was a cranky cat after all. If everybody was nice to her, maybe she'd be nice to them. But then, if SHE was nicer to others, maybe that would make THEM nicer to her. Yes, she thought, that must be the answer. If she changed her own ways, people would like her, wouldn't they?

The tomcat had gone, but the wounds inflicted upon her by Tommy still hurt.

"It's not worth getting hurt like this. Oh dear, I think I'd better change my ways. I'll start right now. I'll do it. I'll go in and be nice and kind to my dear old owner. I can do it, I know I can. After all, I am a clever little cat!"

Creeping out from under the bush, she padded back into the house through her cat-door. Entering the kitchen, she wrapped her black and white body around her owner's leg and mewed gently.

Mrs. Catzenpfeffer gave a gusty sigh, bent down and stroked the little cat. Cranky purred gratefully, and quietly went to curl up in her little bed next to the kitchen stove.

As the days, weeks and many months passed, Cranky practised being nice. It seemed to work. She no longer scratched people who dropped by to visit. She no longer hissed at other creatures in the garden. Cranky became more loveable to everyone, especially the old lady.

One morning Cranky awoke feeling sick and tired. She didn't want to eat or drink. Her eyes looked dull and she felt very ill. Mrs. Catzenpfeffer took Cranky to the vet who proclaimed the little cat was suffering from kidney failure. He told her owner to put a water-drip into the little cat's body to keep her hydrated.

He didn't expect Cranky to make it through this serious illness. Mrs. Catzenpfeffer did everything the vet commanded, but Cranky got more and more ill.

One night, Cranky decided she'd had enough. She slowly arose from her bed by the stove, shook off the water-tube and went out through the cat-door into the garden. She crawled under her favourite bush and waited for the final long sleep to send her up to Kitty Heaven.

Mrs. Catzenpfeffer came downstairs to check on her little cat but found her gone. She went outside calling for Cranky. Soon she heard a soft, pitiful mewing coming from under a bush. She carefully carried Cranky back inside the house and laid her in her bed.

The next morning Mrs. Catzenpfeffer telephoned

the vet. He said it was time for him to come to the
house to give Cranky an injection that would let her
fall asleep forever. He told Mrs. Catzenpfeffer that
he'd be there in an hour or so. The old lady stared
sadly at her pet.

"Cranky, let's go outside for the last time. I'll put a
lead on you and walk you around the flowerbeds for
you to sniff your favourite flowers. I don't want you
running off again, you see." But Mrs. Catzenpfeffer
didn't have a lead because there was no dog in the
house. She took a soft red cotton belt from one of
her trousers, tied it around Cranky's neck and led
her outside.

Cranky moved slowly, dragging her feet, looking
oh-so-tired. She moved from plant to plant, sniffing
here and there, while Mrs. Catzenpfeffer bent to
stroke her furry head from time to time.

Suddenly the tomcat appeared. Tommy leapt down from the fence and rushed at Cranky. She looked up startled. Her back arched. Her hair stood up on end all over her thin, ill, frightened body. She yowled in terror as Tommy bared his teeth in front of her face, hissing horribly.

Cranky gave a huge meowwwwwww, pulled the makeshift lead out of her owner's hand and went at Tommy, hissing and snarling and baring her own teeth. The tomcat looked surprised, turned around, and immediately scampered away. All you could see was his orange tail fast disappearing over the fence.

Cranky meowed quietly, looked triumphantly at the empty fence, and marched strongly back through the open door of the house with her furry head held high.

Mrs. Catzenpfeffer saw that Cranky was now just fine, thank you. She picked up the telephone and told the vet what had happened.

The vet was thoughtfully quiet for a moment. then said down the phone, "I bet I know what happened, Mrs. Catzenpfeffer. Adrenaline poured through your cat's veins and gave her a new lease on life. That adrenaline, you see, is a hormone that is released into the bloodstream when you're scared or suddenly under stress. Well, my dear lady, I won't need to come by after all to put Cranky to sleep, by the sound of it."

"Oh doctor, that is such good news. Cranky has become such a sweet, loving cat over the past year, you know, just not bad-tempered anymore at all."

"Sounds to me you might consider changing her name then, don't you think?" the vet laughed over the phone.

Mrs. Catzenpfeffer put the phone down. Cranky jumped up into her wide lap and began to purr rhythmically.

Kneading her claws gently up and down onto her owner's thighs, Cranky smiled to herself. Her eyebrows seemed to lift away from her nose, parting widely. She no longer wore a sour expression.

"Look at you, you sweetest of cats, you look positively amiable and pleasant. What a good little cat you've turned into, Cranky, my dear. Now, should we think up a new name for you, my little kitty, should we?

Cranky lived happily for a further two years and was never grumpy, mean or bad-tempered ever again.

Can you think up a new name for the sweet little pussy cat?

This is the true story of a Californian farm cat. Names have been changed to protect both human and feline identities.

# ABOUT THE AUTHOR

Shirley Read-Jahn was born during World War II and educated in England before becoming a hippy and living in an ancient Roman burial tomb in Matala, Crete. She went on to take up many different colourful careers, including swimwear model, interpreter, landscape gardener, paralegal and events organiser. She also co-founded the highly-successful San Francisco Jazz Festival as well as running her own landscape business in the United States.

Shirley has belly-danced since her thirties, still plays table-tennis, and now lives in Australia. In retirement, she has finally found time to devote to her passion for writing and the books swirling around in her head.

Email: shirleyreadjahnbooks@gmail.com
Facebook: www.facebook.com/srjpublications/

Join me and other memoir readers and authors in the 'We Love Memoirs' Facebook group, the friendliest group on Facebook.
www.facebook.com/groups/welovememoirs/

**BOOKS FOR CHILDREN**

**The Prince Oliver Penguin Trilogy:**

Volume 1: Prince Oliver and his Friend, Olivia

Volume 2: Olivia and Prince Oliver's Penguins

Volume 3: Prince Oliver & the Penguin Chicks

**Wally the Water Dragon Series:**

Wally and the Mouse

Wally and the Bushfire

Braith the Basset

Hello Snail

Fleur the Flowerpot Possum

Cranky the Cat

**ADULT READING**

Hidden in Plain Sight: A British Military Agent's Story

Dancing through Life: A Memoir, Volume 1

Dancing through Life: A Memoir, Volume 2